I Am MAGICAL!

By: Saieda Salihi

I feel like I am magical, and I can use my magical hands to give everyone a hug!

I am magical because I can use my magical nose to smell beautiful flowers!

I always feel magical when I use my magical eyes to see this amazing world!

I feel amazing when I can use my magical legs to walk, run and play!

I feel so powerful when I can use my magical face to smile and make everyone happy!

I can always use my *magical* fingers to add, subtract and learn all the numbers!

I feel great when I can use my *magical* words to say what I want, and express what I am feeling!

I also feel amazing when I can use my magical heart to love every one around me!

I can use my magical voice to scream yay when I am excited, or lower it when it's time to stay quite.

I feel like I have super powers when use my *magical* brain to learn and teach others.

I feel incredible when I use the *magic* of empathy in me to help someone in need!

I wake up every day feeling *magical* just by being myself. This feeling stays with me, and I continue to be *magical* everywhere I go!

You are Magical!

Everyone is special and magical in their own way! Write a few things that make you feel like you are magical...

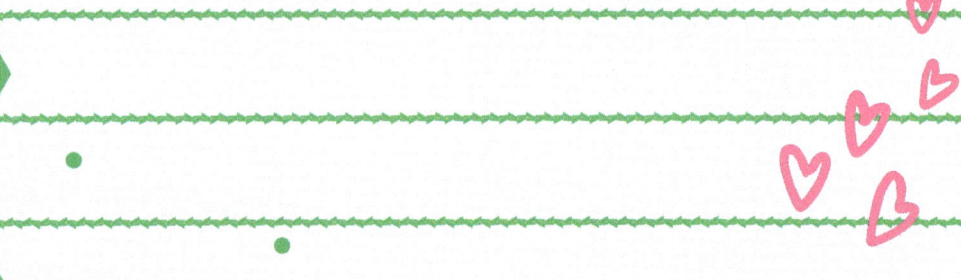

www.ingramcontent.com/pod-product-compliance
Lightning Source LLC
Chambersburg PA
CBHW042033100526
44587CB00029B/4399